NATURE'S IMAGES
of
WHITE ROCK LAKE PARK

George Boyd and Becky Rader

Nature's Images of White Rock Lake Park

Copyright © 2014 by Becky Rader

All rights reserved. No part of this publication may be reproduced, distributed, or transmitted in any form or by any means, including photocopying, recording, or other electronic or mechanical methods, without the prior written permission of the publisher, except in the case of brief quotations embodied in critical reviews and certain other noncommercial uses permitted by copyright law. For permission requests, write to the publisher's representative at the address below.

Mary Beth Smith
Park Cities Publishing
3032 Mockingbird Lane
Dallas, TX 75205

Ordering Information:
Quantity sales. Special discounts are available on quantity purchases by corporations, associations, and others. For details, contact the publisher at the address above.

Printed in the United States of America

This book is dedicated to
George and Shirley Boyd

white rock LAKE MAP

Legend:
- Boat Ramp
- Water Fountain
- Restrooms
- Parking Area
- Wildflower Area
- Hike & Bike Trail
- Access to Lake
- Paved Roads
- Hatchery/Dam/Spillway
- Park Office
- Playground

Map labels:
- northwest hwy.
- mockingbird ln.
- MOCKINGBIRD LOT
- buckner blvd
- doran cir.
- PARK OFFICE FOR RESERVATIONS
- RUNNERS' LOT
- w. lawther
- CYCLISTS' LOT
- NORTHCLIFF
- lake highlands
- BATH HOUSE LOT
- JACKSON POINT
- STONE TABLES
- Poppy
- BOAT LAUNCHING LOT
- WINFREY POINT
- Emerald Isle
- garland rd.
- Williamson
- BOAT HOUSE
- E. Lawther
- SPILLWAY
- SPILLWAY LOT
- winsted
- gaston ave.
- N

MAP COURTESY OF **ADVOCATE** BE LOCAL

GARLAND RD. ACCESS
1. South Entrance to Park
2. Dallas Arboretum

E. LAWTHER/EMERALD ISLE ACCESS from Garland Rd.
3. MultiStation Outdoor Workout Center
4. Civilian Conservation Corps Camp
5. Winfrey Point

NORTHCLIFF/ POPPY/ LAKE HIGHLANDS ACCESS
6. Sunset Bay, CCC Statue
7. Dreyfuss Club
8. Bath House Cultural Center, White Rock Lake Museum

E. LAWTHER ACCESS from Mockingbird
9. Corinthian Sailing Club
10. Scenic View & Photographic Opportunity
11. Big Thicket
12. White Rock Boat Club

NW HWY ACCESS
13. Flagpole Hill

W. LAWTHER ACCESS
14. Mount Vernon
15. TP Hill, Boat House
16. Pump Station
17. Fish Hatchery & Nature Trail Entrance

GARLAND RD. ACCESS
18. Spillway
19. YMCA at White Rock

iv

PREFACE

The purpose of this book is to introduce the reader to the natural aspect of White Rock Lake Park, representative of the entire North Central Texas region. White Rock Creek is a direct link to the Trinity River. Its headwaters are located at a spring in Frisco, Texas and from there it flows and adds to the waters of White Rock Lake before continuing to the river.

The primary use is for families and others who are unfamiliar with the plants and urban wildlife, the flora and fauna, which make up the existing habitat in our area.

This book is not intended to be a replacement for a field guide that goes into more detail about flora and fauna species. Instead it can be used as a primer on lake and regional inhabitants.

The photos were all taken by George Boyd over a period of almost 30 years, beginning in the mid 1980's. The immediate White Rock Lake Park area was the only location used for the photography of this book

A journal page is included where children, and adults, can begin recording the birds, mammals, reptiles, amphibians, butterflies, dragonflies, and prairie wildflowers they recognize from this book and see at the lake and other nearby areas. It is the hope of the authors that you will have the opportunity to see them all.

Table of Contents

Map of White Rock Lake .... *iv*

Preface .... *v*

Introduction 1

Chapter 1 - Food 3

Chapter 2 - Water 27

Chapter 3 - Cover and Raising Young 53

Chapter 4 - Colors 73

Chapter 5 - Infrequent and Unusual Visitors 85

Checklist 95

Glossary 97

Resources 99

Special Thanks 101

About the Authors 103

Special Note 107

Northern Bobwhite Quail *(Colinus virginianus)*

INTRODUCTION

Wildlife has found a perfect place in White Rock Lake Park. It provides everything that is needed for them to survive there, the food, water, cover and a safe place to raise their young, all creating a perfect habitat.

Not all the plants are native, but the wildlife has had almost 100 years to adapt to the plants around the lake and in our yards too. That is the urban part of the place we all live in.

Gone are the 12,000,000 acres of Blackland Prairie that once existed here in Texas. That soil was too rich for farmers to resist and cotton became king when the plow turned the soil and the prairie vanished.

There are still small places, called remnants, of that great prairie that reached from San Antonio all the way to Canada. Some of those remnants still exist at the lake because the soil was too shallow for crops and the chalk rock too close to the surface. From bison to cattle, the land was grazed before the lake was built. A bison skull was found in Dixon Branch Creek, near the lake, by SMU archeologists in the 1940's.

There are memories from local residents of hunting here in the 1940's for turkey and quail around the lake. Both Becky and George have seen Bobwhite Quail here, but it was many years ago. Last time Becky saw any was a covey of quail at Norbuck Park in 1990. George even has a picture of one taken at Boy Scout Hill in the 1980's. He said that was the beginning of the interest in birds for him. See his photo following.

Over the years the land the park is on has changed from an open prairie with a tree lined creek to a forested landscape and lake created by man's hand. The change has brought about an increase in the number and variety of wildlife that can survive and adapt in our urban environment.

Take a look at some of our wildlife that make the lake their home.

Chapter 1

FOOD

Food for wildlife can be any number of things. The following photos show the variety of species that flock to one species of tree, the Red Mulberry, and its ripe juicy berries.

Plus there are the mast bearing trees producing pecans, acorns, and walnuts for the Squirrels, Raccoons and more.

And lest we not forget, there are the seeds from the grasses and wildflowers for our over wintering species, like the Harris's Sparrow.

Or the wetland foods, like frogs and crawdads --- or crayfish or mud bugs or crawfish --- whatever you grew up calling them, provided for the Mink, Herons and others.

What about the fish out in that lake? Seems there are a few birds and animals that like a nice bass or sunfish every now and then, like the Great Blue Heron, the White Pelicans and Mink.

Just thinking about all the different opportunities and wide variety of food that this area has to offer the wildlife here, from prairies, to wetlands, to forest and deep water it is a smorgasbord of plenty.

And with that platter of plenty, those that feed and live here provide food for the predators that follow the crowd. It is a very delicate connection, that web of life that continues to intrigue us all.

White Rock Lake allows us an up close look at that connection every day, if we take the time to look.

But a few reminders first…

NATURE'S IMAGES *of* WHITE ROCK LAKE PARK

Rules of wildlife viewing:

- Keep your distance
- Be quiet
- Move slowly
- Do not disturb

If you see an injured or sick animal…do not attempt to pick it up. Call DFW Wildlife Coalition, see the reference page, to report it and follow their advice.

Never, never ever feed the wildlife at the lake! That is dangerous for you and for them. They have lots of great food fresh from nature that is much better for them to eat.

Do not attempt to get close for the benefit of a better picture. Stay safe and at a distance.

If you see a baby bird, do not pick it up, call DFW Wildlife Coalition and ask for assistance. They will provide you with the information you need.

Safety is the first priority when it comes to viewing the wildlife at the lake…. yours and the critters that live there. Be smart, think before you act.

Remember this –

All migratory birds, including raptors, are protected under the Migratory Bird Treaty Act which is enforced by the US Fish and Wildlife Service and the Texas Parks and Wildlife Department.

Texas State Laws prohibit the capture or possession of any non-game species of wildlife without a permit.

And now, time to get out there for a look!

CHAPTER 1 - FOOD

Cedar Waxwings *(Bombycilla cedrorum)*
Red Mulberry *(Morus Rubra)*

The Banquet is Now Open

The Red Mulberry tree at Boy Scout Hill is a bonanza of food for the birds and other wildlife at the lake.

George has great stories of all the times he has taken up a spot there with his camera on the ready to capture the banquet in full swing.

NATURE'S IMAGES *of* WHITE ROCK LAKE PARK

Cedar Waxwings *(Bombycilla cedrorum)*

Sharing :)

They are small but beautiful birds that are seen here during the winter months, usually in large flocks.

You just might have had the unfortunate occurrence of parking under a tree where they briefly roost, which will mean your car needs a bath.

CHAPTER 1 - FOOD

Male Baltimore Oriole *(Icterus galbula)*

I Pick This One

Enjoying the fruits of the mulberry, quite juicy and sweet, but very messy.

People can eat them also.

Orioles are beautiful birds not seen very often in our area. They enjoy caterpillars, fruit and nectar. They can be seen nesting in the Mulberry tree.

NATURE'S IMAGES *of* WHITE ROCK LAKE PARK

Red-shouldered Hawk *(Buteo lineatus)*

All Right You Dirty Rat…Take That!

Yes, he caught dinner. Not the prettiest sight but glad there is one less rat. Rodents make up a large part of any raptor's diet, from rabbits and squirrels to mice and rats; they are all on the menu.

This hawk has beautiful orange barring on the chest and red colored shoulder patches.

George watched as this hawk consumed his meal, one bite at a time.

CHAPTER 1 - FOOD

Yellow-crowned Night-Heron *(Nyctanassa violacea)*

Crawdad for Dinner!

George was lucky to see this one during the daylight hours. They forage mainly at night for crawdads in swampy areas and along covered shorelines. Hidden in trees are large colonies where they will nest. No nesting colonies at the lake, but they do feed here then return to their nesting site elsewhere.

You can see the feather plumes on the back of this one's head along with the big white cheek patches. Tall grey bird with yellow legs….how dashing!

NATURE'S IMAGES *of* WHITE ROCK LAKE PARK

Eastern Phoebe *(Sayornis phoebe)*

Now That's A Mouthful!

Catches flying insects like this dragonfly. When perched it will wag its tail!

These are small birds that will consume many large insects just like we see here.

CHAPTER 1 - FOOD

Sharp-shinned Hawk *(Accipiter striatus)* and Blue Jay mob

Leave Me Alone

He missed. Other birds will gang up on a raptor to defend their territory. This mobbing behavior is especially common with Blue Jays.

NATURE'S IMAGES *of* WHITE ROCK LAKE PARK

American Kestrel *(Falco sparverius)*

Balancing Act

These are beautiful small raptors that are often seen hunting at the lake in open grassland areas for insects and small mammals. This one has caught a grasshopper for a snack. Pairs will nest in tree cavities.

CHAPTER 1 - FOOD

Male American Kestrel *(Falco sparverius)*

Do You Mind?

I believe that George told me this one actually caught a small bird and was caught eating it high up in the branches of a tree. This is something that is not often witnessed by anyone. Glad George was there to actually see this and capture the moment with his camera.

The markings on the Kestrel are beautiful!

Mink *(Mustela vison)*

Hurry, Hurry, Makes It Blurry, Blurry!

What a lucky shot this one was for George. Seeing and actually photographing one of the most elusive inhabitants of the lake was a real prize. It looks like this Mink has nabbed a big crawdad and is running off with it for dinner time. He is running so fast he is nothing but a blur, but George was still able to catch him.

Mink had not been seen at the lake until George photographed them. Great discovery! They live near water and will hunt almost anything and fear nothing.

CHAPTER 1 - FOOD

Great Horned Owl *(Bubo virginianus)*
Eastern Fox Squirrel *(Sciurus niger Linnaeus)*

Come A Little Bit Closer…

Great shot showing predator and prey. It looks like that squirrel is living just a tad bit on the dangerous side. Or maybe the Owl is being so still the Squirrel does not see him….yet. Makes you wonder what happened next, doesn't it?

The Great Horned owls are some of the earliest nesting raptors, beginning in December. They are monogamous and will nest in the same site each year. Not really ears or horns but tufts of feathers giving them their name. They are the largest of the different owl species at the lake.

NATURE'S IMAGES *of* WHITE ROCK LAKE PARK

Coopers Hawk *(Accipiter cooperii)*
American Coot *(Fulica americana)*

Wow! Can't Believe I Caught A Coot!

The captured coot is identified by the lobed toes and green color.

Excellent timing for George who was there at the very instant the Cooper's hawk swooped down and caught the Coot at the Spillway.

There has been a nesting pair at the lake for several years now and nesting had not been recorded in Dallas County until the 1990's by Audubon members.

CHAPTER 1 - FOOD

Gulf Fritillary *(Agraulis vanillae incarnata)*
Tropical Sage *(Salvia coccinea)*

So Thirsty!

Gorgeous butterfly that is very common at the lake. They are considered pollinators also. Nectar is the food of choice and necessity due to the straw-like proboscis. Note that the underside of the wing is completely different than the top side.

You think birds are difficult to photograph, try chasing down butterflies and holding your breath hoping they won't fly off. This according to George!

NATURE'S IMAGES *of* WHITE ROCK LAKE PARK

Question Mark *(Polygonia interrogationis)*
Basket-Flower *(Centaurea americana)*

You Can't See Me, Right?

Beautiful photo showing the wings and body of the butterfly in complete contrast to the color of the flower it has landed on and is gathering nectar from.

CHAPTER 1 - FOOD

Male Ruby-throated Hummingbird *(Archilochus colubris)*
Turk's Cap *(Malvaviscus Drummondii)*

Need More Fuel!

Wings are a blur here, but they are there!

This photo catches him in the act of feeding from a Turk's Cap flower using his long bill and tongue to reach for the nectar held in the bloom. There might be some small tasty insect morsels in there too, just an added bonus for this dazzling hummer.

NATURE'S IMAGES *of* WHITE ROCK LAKE PARK

Pipevine Swallowtail *(Battus p. philenor)*
Pickerelweed *(Pontederia cordata)*

So Good, So Good!

Love the colors; purple, blue, orange, white and the background of green. All butterflies are excellent pollinators for the plants.

CHAPTER 1 - FOOD

Monarch *(Danaus p. plexippus)*
White Boneset *(Eupatorium serotinum)*

All Mine!

If you are lucky, you will see the Monarchs making a stopover at the lake during fall migration on their way to Mexico for the winter. It is an amazing sight! George was once again at the right place at the right time!

Monarchs are the State Butterfly of Texas. :)

Cedar Waxwing *(Bombycilla cedorum)*

Umm, Umm Good!

This photo is included to show that in spite of the invasive nature of some introduced plants they do serve a purpose. Birds will take advantage of food no matter if it is a native or non-native plant. To them food is food.

What native to this area, that is an evergreen understory shrub, will provide the same type of food for birds, nectar for bees, leaves for caterpillars and cover for several wildlife species if the privet is removed? Something to consider.

Land management in an urban environment is a complex issue.

Harris's Sparrow *(Zonotrichia querula)*

It's Stuck, Help!

This is just one of the many small native sparrow species that visit the lake. Here it is taking advantage of a juicy morsel.

The Harris's over winters here staying in the thickets and shrubby areas. This is the largest native sparrow at 7.5" long.

NATURE'S IMAGES *of* WHITE ROCK LAKE PARK

Dickcissel *(Spiza Americana)*

I See You

A great sighting by George. They are not seen very often at the lake. Dickcissels feed on grass seed and are found in the tallgrass prairie areas.

CHAPTER 1 - FOOD

American White Pelicans *(Pelecanus erythrorhynchos)*

The Feast of Fish

These pelicans just completed herding a shoal of fish towards the shoreline which made it easy pickings for them, more than likely some sunfish or shad. If you look closely you can see some in the bills and pouches of the pelicans.

Pelicans will work together to acquire food as shown here. It is almost like a well choreographed dance, each one synchronized with the other swimming and dipping heads in the water in unison.

NATURE'S IMAGES *of* WHITE ROCK LAKE PARK

Great Blue Heron *(Ardea Herodias)*

Good Catch!

The heron will flip the fish up so that it will be swallowed head first. That is quite a catch that any fisherman would be proud of.

The Great Blue Heron is the largest of the herons at 46" in length. The gray color and dark crown are unmistakable.

Chapter 2

WATER

Water seems to be everywhere; this is after all White Rock Lake we are talking about. But did you know that the headwaters for White Rock Creek are in Frisco beginning at a small spring? Several other springs and creeks join to provide the continuous flow of water this lake provides for our enjoyment, recreation and for the wildlife too. It is one of the main tributaries for the Trinity River.

Wildlife finds several locations of water in this park. There are creeks flowing into the lake that are used as wildlife corridors, or connections, to other areas. The Old Fish Hatchery, consisting of several ponds, is another area that though man-made is an excellent location to find several species of wildlife. During drought most of those ponds dry up and only a few retain water. The photos from George show them full of water.

Because of the water, food and cover, White Rock Lake is an integral stopover for migrating waterfowl and songbirds during the spring and fall months at the height of migration. This area is part of the Central Flyway Migratory Route that the migrating birds use as they travel from South and Central America to the northern parts of the United States or Canada in the spring and vice versa in the fall.

Some species like the hummingbirds will travel thousands of miles from South America across the Gulf of Mexico to Texas where they will nest and raise their young before the return journey in the fall to warmer climes.

Other wildlife are year-round residents here because of the water source. Some of those are the Mallard ducks, Cardinals, Mockingbirds, Owls, Mink, Beaver, and Squirrels for example.

There are some species that are winter residents like the Pelicans and native sparrows. Take a look at the following photos from George.

Beaver Dam in the Old Fish Hatchery area

Beaver Dam

This dam has been there a very long time. George says to look closely at this photo and you will see a "huge wild climbing rose blooming. This was flooded and sadly the rose died."

The Old Fish Hatchery is a wonderful place to explore. There are a few benches where you can sit and enjoy listening to the birds.

CHAPTER 2 - WATER

Beaver *(Castor canadensis)*

What You Lookin At?

This Beaver didn't stick around long according to George, "One minute he was there and then he was gone."

George's story,"The Beaver was at the creek where it was dammed up, he was taking a look at me, kinda played hide and see. I had to clip some vines out of the way to get a good picture, got the picture – then he swam right by me, too close to focus."

NATURE'S IMAGES *of* WHITE ROCK LAKE PARK

Red-eared Sliders *(Trachemys scripta elegans)*

Love That Sun!

This old fallen tree trunk provides the perfect sunning spot for this bunch of turtles to sun on. Plenty of room for all it looks like, large and small.

The Red-eared Slider is just an example of several of the turtle species at the lake. They feed mainly on aquatic plants but will also eat fish and carrion in the water.

CHAPTER 2 - WATER

Common Snapping Turtle *(Chelydra serpentina serpentina)*

Don't Even Think About It

George saw this one crawling up on a mud bank out of one of the ponds. With that look, I bet he gave him a wide berth.

Snapping turtles have a very long neck and can reach almost to their back legs. Not a good idea to ever try to pick one up.

They are active predators in the water on fish, ducklings, frogs, and more.

Copperhead *(Agkistrodon contortrix)*

Watch Where You're Walkin!

This photo was taken at the Old Fish Hatchery Ponds, this from George, "I was following a Cooper's Hawk sitting on a limb near some herons. I took the picture and heard a loud expletive. A man came up and said he almost stepped on a snake. He showed me the picture. I had just walked no more than a foot from that snake and didn't know it was there. I went back to the same spot where I took his picture. " Lucky George.

As George told me when we looked at this, "It was a pretty good sized snake." I agree!

CHAPTER 2 - WATER

Green Treefrog *(Hyla cinerea)*

Green on Green

It took some sharp eyes to see this little frog clinging to the side of a cattail. This is a frog common to swamps, creeks, rivers or edges of lakes, if there is the dense vegetation it requires for habitat.

The Green Treefrog eats insects and will hide under leaves if threatened.

NATURE'S IMAGES *of* WHITE ROCK LAKE PARK

Pair of Mink at the pond

Making A Mad Dash

This is perfect habitat for the mink at one of the Old Fish Hatchery ponds. It is the right combination of water, food source, and cover for protection and den sites for them.

They obviously do not like having their picture taken!

Male Wood Duck *(Aix sponsa)*

Handsome Indeed!

The most gorgeous of our native ducks, don't you agree?

What is unusual about them is that they nest in tree cavities or specially built boxes near sheltered ponds, like this part of the park, to raise their young.

Instead of feeding on vegetation like many other species of duck, the Wood duck is fond of acorns and other seeds.

NATURE'S IMAGES *of* WHITE ROCK LAKE PARK

Green Heron *(Butorides virescens)*

I See It, Wait For It …

This is a small and secretive heron that inhabits the edges of swampy areas. Its dark coloration lends to hiding in shadows of wooded ponds where it feeds on fish.

A wonderful photo showing the long neck of this Green Heron. Wonder if he caught that fish or maybe a frog? What do you think?

CHAPTER 2 - WATER

Diamond-backed Watersnake *(Nerodia rhombifer)*

Whew, Almost There

Yes, there are snakes at the lake and more non-venomous than venomous ones. This one is beautifully colored and the pattern on his back denotes the name Diamond-backed watersnake, non-venomous.

The ability to swim without legs or feet is truly amazing. By the undulations of the body the snake is able to swim above and under the water. The prey of water snakes is toads, frogs, and fish.

NATURE'S IMAGES *of* WHITE ROCK LAKE PARK

Great Egrets *(Ardea alba)*
Snowy Egrets *(Egretta thula)*
Roseate Spoonbill *(Platalea ajaja)*

Did Someone Say Heads Up or Heads Down?

The spillway is an excellent viewing spot for a number of waterfowl. The algae growing there attract a wide assortment of small crustaceans and invertebrates for these hungry birds. Fish, tadpoles and frogs will be gobbled up by this assembly of keen eyed birds also.

Looks like George caught the Roseate Spoonbill busy at work seining the water with his specialized bill for food.

Beautiful pink coloration on the Spoonbill, think the others might be a little it jealous?

CHAPTER 2 - WATER

American White Pelicans *(Pelicanus erythrorhynchos)*

All Together…Now!

Great photo showing the fishing techniques the Pelicans use when surrounding a school of fish. It is a group effort. Love that leg in the air too! What finesse.

Our lake is a wonderful winter paradise for the Pelicans and their arrival is looked forward to by many every year.

NATURE'S IMAGES *of* WHITE ROCK LAKE PARK

Another Pelican in action

Landing Gear Down

The wingspan of an adult Pelican is 9 feet. And they can weigh 16 pounds. Now that's a lot of bird to get in the air and then to land. That's something isn't it?

Beautiful approach and just look at those wings!

CHAPTER 2 - WATER

Same bird in previous photo as he lands in the water.

Splashdown

These two pictures show this pelican's beautiful descent upon the lake. Wonderful action photos!

Nothing like a little barefoot skiing! Time to find some lunch!

Snowy Egrets *(Egretta thula)*

Water Ballet

This is a favorite photo of many of George's fans. The shadow on the wings and the sparkle of the water makes it seem as if they are truly dancing right in front of you. George says to look at the water droplets dripping from the toes….

CHAPTER 2 - WATER

Northern Pintail *(Anas acuta)*

Not Any Closer

Pintails are just one of many winter visitors to the lake. During the breeding season the male will have long tail feathers, that is how they got the name.

They graze on plants and seeds. Nesting occurs from the tip of the Panhandle all the way up into far northern Canada.

NATURE'S IMAGES *of* WHITE ROCK LAKE PARK

Spotted Sandpiper *(Actitis macularia)*

Never-ending Search

George saw this one near the Fruiting Mulberry Tree on the shoreline near Boy Scout Hill. It is looking for some good nibbles in the crevices and cracks of rocks along the shoreline.

CHAPTER 2 - WATER

Bobcat *(Lynx rufus)*

Wait…That's Not a Duck!

Yes, when a bobcat wants to avoid you, like always, they will go far out of their way to do that…..like swimming away.

George saw this one near Sunset Bay swimming across to find some well deserved privacy. It can be tough on the wildlife when there is a lot of activity at the lake and they have young to feed. They have learned to adapt to living in the urban environment and it is rare that you will see one.

NATURE'S IMAGES *of* WHITE ROCK LAKE PARK

White Ibis *(Eudocimus albus)*

My What Pretty Legs…

This is an adult with white plumage and bright pink facial skin. The White Ibis is rarely seen here. It is much more common in coastal areas.

CHAPTER 2 - WATER

Little Blue Heron *(Egretta caerulea)*

My What Long Toes You have....

Notice the beautifully unique coloration of the breeding plumage as seen here. The head and neck are a reddish-purple, the body a slate blue, and legs and feet are black.

Hooded Mergansers *(Lophodytes cucullatus)*

Lookin' Handsome for the Ladies

This is another winter visitor that likes ponds near woods and dead trees with cavities. Here it can be found in the sheltered areas of the lake protected by trees and other vegetation along the shoreline.

It feeds in shallow waters and their diet consists of insects, crustaceans and small fish. Both male and female have a crest, the male has a brilliant white stripe on the crest and white on the breast.

CHAPTER 2 - WATER

Belted Kingfisher *(Ceryle alcyon)*

Here Fishy, Fishy

The most common Kingfisher in North America. Both the male and female have the blue band on the breast. Females only have a rust belly band.

Black-crowned Night-Heron *(Nycticorax nycticorax)*

This Is My Good Side

You can barely see one of the long white feathers that extends from the back of the crown towards the back of the bird.

As the name states, this heron is seen mainly at night foraging for its prey along the edges of water. It usually remains in a hunched over position.

CHAPTER 2 - WATER

American Widgeon *(Anus americana)*

Follow the Leader

Winter visitors that will remain until spring then fly north for the breeding season. This pretty duck feeds on surface aquatic vegetation and will also graze on the shore if undisturbed.

The males are easily recognized by the white forehead and the dark colored feathers around the eye blending into an iridescent green on the back of the head.

It is time to invest in a good pair of binoculars and a long lens for your camera to catch these.

NATURE'S IMAGES *of* WHITE ROCK LAKE PARK

Black-bellied Whistling-Ducks *(Dendrocygna autumnalis)*

Am I the Only One Awake?

The contrast between the pink legs and the red bill is a real eye catcher. Plus there is the black belly that really makes these ducks standout in a crowd.

This duck is a year round resident and nests in tree cavities or duck boxes located near water. Their food source is seeds from plants in the water, along the edge or in fields.

They have a whistling call and that is why it is part of their very descriptive name.

Chapter 3

COVER AND RAISING YOUNG

Cover and Raising Young- it is not possible to have one without the other. For wildlife to raise young they need shelter or cover for protection. Each species has different requirements for reproduction and providing for the offspring.

Some species of birds like to nest in the hollows or cavities of trees, like owls, bluebirds, and woodpeckers found in the canopy area. Some birds require the middle of the forest to nest in understory trees and shrubs, like the cardinals and hummingbirds. Fox, coyote, bobcat, armadillos and many more choose to dig dens under the shrubs for protection and a secure place for raising their young.

The areas of tallgrass remnants provide nesting sites for the Red-winged blackbirds who use the grass blades to weave a nest suspended off the ground. Rabbits will make a hollow in the tall grass covered by a mound of grass for their nesting and resting sites.

Turtles will leave the water, dig a hole to deposit their eggs, cover it up to stay warm and dry, and leave for the babies to hatch on their own. Killdeer nest in short grass or rocky areas of the soil where their spotted eggs are camouflaged. The birds protect the nest by leading a possible predator away pretending to have a broken wing. The distraction saves the eggs and babies from predation.

Even the plants provide for the insects we see. Butterflies, crickets, grasshoppers and more feed on the plants and lay their eggs on certain plants, like the Monarch and Milkweed, or the Swallowtail and Wild Carrot. Others lay their eggs in the soil near the plants to ensure food for the hatched young.

From the top of the forest canopy to the prairie and bare ground, each area provides cover and a safe place for wildlife to raise their young at the lake.

George has been able to witness and document many of the young wildlife at the lake for close to 30 years and now you can too. Turn the page…

NATURE'S IMAGES *of* WHITE ROCK LAKE PARK

Red-shouldered Hawk pair and two babies *(Buteo lineatus)*

Go Away!

Raptors are very protective of their nesting sites. Do not disturb!

CHAPTER 3 - COVER AND RAISING YOUNG

Juvenile White Ibis *(Eudocimus albus)*

Looking for Lunch

Not yet in the full white plumage he will develop as an adult, but still a beauty. The bill that is now orange will become a vibrant red-orange color as he matures.

NATURE'S IMAGES *of* WHITE ROCK LAKE PARK

Female Wood Duck with ducklings *(Aix sponsa)*

Single File

Raising young at the lake in the middle of this urban environment is extremely difficult for wildlife. Remember to watch, but leave alone and do not disturb with loud noise or fast movements. Be respectful.

CHAPTER 3 - COVER AND RAISING YOUNG

Barred Owl youngsters *(Strix varia)*

Peeking Out

The pair of Barred Owl adults at this site raised several young through the years. George was able to document them as they grew. Cute aren't they?

Baltimore Oriole *(Icterus galbula)* nest

Feeding Time

The babies need a high protein diet so will be fed tasty insects and caterpillars as they continue to grow.

The nests are woven and hang from the branches. Very adept nest builders don't you think? Just look at what was used to make this one. Do you recognize that green stuff?

Look very closely and you can also see a very dangerous addition to the nest construction…fishing line, or monofilament line, that could potentially get tangled around the parent or the babies. If you see any while at the lake, please pick it up and dispose of it properly, the wildlife thanks you very much. :)

CHAPTER 3 - COVER AND RAISING YOUNG

Raccoon babies *(Procyon lotor)*

Your caption here...

The Raccoon adults took over an owl nesting site for their own babies.

NATURE'S IMAGES *of* WHITE ROCK LAKE PARK

Mink babies *(Mustela vison)*

Wrestle Mania

George was quick to capture these two playing on the trail. He said they scampered off as soon as they saw him. He was able to get 3 different photos of them wrestling around before they went back into the cover of the understory shrubs.

CHAPTER 3 - COVER AND RAISING YOUNG

Can you find what is hiding here?

Great camouflage. Hint…it is an insect.

NATURE'S IMAGES *of* WHITE ROCK LAKE PARK

Eastern Cottontail *(Sylvilagus floridanus)*

Hiding

Rabbits will freeze if they believe there is danger nearby. This allows them to be undetected by many predators. The tall prairie grasses and shrub thickets are a great place for them to find food, provide cover and a safe place to raise their young.

CHAPTER 3 - COVER AND RAISING YOUNG

Young Coyote *(Canis latrans)*

Curious

Hey, wanna play?

Remember to stay away if you see coyotes. Make loud noises to scare them so they do not approach people.

NATURE'S IMAGES *of* WHITE ROCK LAKE PARK

Virginia Opossum *(Didelphis virginiana)*

Climbing Tree

The Opossum is the only marsupial in North America. Who remembers what a marsupial is? Most of them live in Australia.

CHAPTER 3 - COVER AND RAISING YOUNG

Green Tree Frog *(Hyla cinerea)*
Cattail *(Typha sp.)*

The Golden Arch

Cattails provide cover for this little frog and protection from hungry birds.

NATURE'S IMAGES *of* WHITE ROCK LAKE PARK

Male Red-winged Blackbird *(Agelaius phoeniceus)*
Arkansas Yucca *(Yucca arkansana)*

My Territory…Keep Out!

This male Red-winged Blackbird is staking out his territory and letting everyone know about it.

Pair of Scissor-tailed Flycatchers *(Tyrannus forficatus)*
Arkansas Yucca *(Yucca arkansana)*

Only Room For One

A pair of one of the most beautiful, acrobatic fliers at the lake.

NATURE'S IMAGES *of* WHITE ROCK LAKE PARK

Male Northern Cardinal and juvenile *(Cardinalis cardinalis)*

More Please!

Lots of cover is needed for nesting sites as well as a food source to provide for the young.

This young cardinal is feathered enough to begin learning about flying, a fledgling. Maybe he is getting some helpful instruction from Dad. Or maybe he is asking for another bite to eat.

If you see a young feathered bird on the ground….leave it alone. This is the stage when the parents still feed them, but they are also learning to fly. They know how to hide and the parents stay nearby to protect them.

CHAPTER 3 - COVER AND RAISING YOUNG

Baby Mallards *(Anas platyrhynchos)*

Look What I Found

These two cuties are probably following the example of their mother as she is grazing the grass and eating fallen fruit under the Red Mulberry tree that attracts so many birds.

Their seemingly mottled coloration is very effective camouflage making them harder to be seen by predators.

NATURE'S IMAGES *of* WHITE ROCK LAKE PARK

Coyotes *(Canis latrans)*

Hide Out

George's photo shows a wonderful example of the kind of cover necessary for the wildlife at the lake. Heavy vegetation like this is beneficial for cover, shelter and successful rearing of the young.

The coloration of the coyotes, though varied in tones of dark and light, aids in their ability to remain camouflaged in the shrubs.

More often than not, you were probably near coyotes when out at the lake and never knew about it. They are fairly secretive in their movements and do not prefer to be near humans.

CHAPTER 3 - COVER AND RAISING YOUNG

Adult and young Coyote *(Canis latrans)*

Time to Come Inside Now

Makes you think this youngster is not too happy with what his parent just said. How many times has that happened to you?

Just like human parents with their children, wildlife young have to learn to listen for their own protection. There are many dangers they have to learn about in order to survive.

Green Anole *(Anolis carolinensis)*

Really! You Can Still See Me?

This familiar lizard is in the process of altering its coloration to adapt to the color of the leaf it is on. The legs are still slightly green while most of the body is now a yellowish –brown, like the leaf. Great camouflage!

Chapter 4

COLOR

Colors of many insects that abound at the lake will amaze you. Can you guess which ones George decided to try and photograph? Here are just a few of those little shimmering insect beauties, plus a couple of other additional winged jewels.

Red Admiral *(Vanessa atalanta)*
Roughleaf Dogwood *(Cornus drummondii)*

Love That Nectar!

The Red Admiral is one of the first butterflies seen in the Spring.

NATURE'S IMAGES *of* WHITE ROCK LAKE PARK

Eastern Black Swallowtail *(Papilio polyxenes asterius)*
Purple Coneflower *(Echinacea angustifolia)*

Any Left?

The purple coneflower has finished blooming and will go to seed so there will be more plants next year.

Black swallowtails are fairly common to see in our area. Incredible coloration.

CHAPTER 4 - COLOR

Orange Sulphur *(Colias eurytheme)*
Texas Aster *(Aster texanus)*

Hang On For More!

A nice close-up of these, which are actually much smaller than shown.

NATURE'S IMAGES *of* WHITE ROCK LAKE PARK

American Lady *(Vanessa verginiensis)*
Gayfeather *(Liatris sp.)*

Look at that Design!

Have you ever seen anything so beautiful with colors, circles, and lines on one insect?

CHAPTER 4 - COLOR

Gray Hairstreak *(Strymon melinus franki)*
Firewheel *(Gaillardia sp.)*

Getting the Last Drop

Gorgeous little butterfly that tricks birds by its mimicry. The ends of the wings resemble the eye and antennae fooling the bird and allowing the butterfly to escape. Isn't nature grand?

NATURE'S IMAGES *of* **WHITE ROCK LAKE PARK**

Female Widow Skimmer *(Libellula luctuosa)*
Virginia wild rye *(Elymus virginicus)*

Up Close and Personal

Frozen for that split second... just long enough for George to snap the picture.

CHAPTER 4 - COLOR

Female Eastern Pondhawk *(Erythemis simplicicollis)*
Cattail *(Typha sp.)*

Resting

Dragonflies are excellent predators of mosquitoes. They are great fun to watch and have dazzling colors.

George certainly had a keen eye to catch them as they rested. Now hold still.

NATURE'S IMAGES *of* WHITE ROCK LAKE PARK

Male Eastern Pondhawk *(Erythemis simplicicollis)*
Water-Primrose *(Ludwigia octovalvis)*

Time To Take-Off

Love this pale blue color. He blends into the sky - wonder why?

CHAPTER 4 - COLOR

Male Neon Skimmer *(Libellula croceipennis)*
Car antenna

What You Lookin At?

Guess this skimmer couldn't find a better place to perch than the antenna on George's car.

Female Ruby-throated Hummingbird *(Archilochus colubris)*
Turk's Cap *(Malvaviscus Drummondii)*

So Many Choices

Females make nests about the size of a quarter. The speed of their flapping wings is incredible, up to 70 times per second!

The need to stay constantly fueled is great due to the high amount of energy that is required for them to be able to fly as they do. "Eat like a bird" does not apply to hummingbirds.

CHAPTER 4 - COLOR

Black- chinned Hummingbird *(Archilochus alexandri)*

In Mid Air

Black-chinned Hummingbirds are becoming more common in our area. The males have a distinctive purple and black throat.

Chapter 5

INFREQUENT AND UNUSUAL VISITORS

There are always a few wildlife visitors to the lake that are not often seen or are unusual. Here are a few that George was able to capture with his camera.

Male Cinnamon Teal *(Anas cyanoptera)*

An infrequent visitor to the lake that is native to North America. They are usually seen in pairs with the Blue-winged Teal.

Spice Finch or Nutmeg Mannikin *(Lonchura punctulata)*

This Spice Finch is a non-native species that was probably an escaped pet or was released. It is a popular bird species in the pet trade.

CHAPTER 5 - INFREQUENT AND UNUSUAL VISITORS

Eurasian Collared-Dove *(Streptopelia decaocto)*

These doves began as escaped or released pets and have now adapted, multiplied and are competing with the native Mourning Doves for habitat. They are native to Europe.

NATURE'S IMAGES *of* WHITE ROCK LAKE PARK

Gray Fox *(Urocyon cinereoargenteus)*

This little native fox is very common to our area but is almost never seen. They are preyed upon by larger predators so remain out of sight most of the time.

The gray fox has a unique ability to climb trees which helps it to escape some predators and also to find prey.

CHAPTER 5 - INFREQUENT AND UNUSUAL VISITORS

Bald Eagle *(Haliaeetus leucocephalus)*
American Crow *(Corvus brachyrhynchos)*

Do you wonder if this crow is having second thoughts about harassing a Bald Eagle? Not a very good idea.

The Bald Eagles have been seen visiting the north end of the lake and the Sunset Bay area in the past. Very exciting to watch when one is at the lake.

Bald Eagle *(Haliaeetus leucocephalus)*

Another great photo by George! The Bald Eagle is an occasional visitor to the lake, usually during the fall or spring.

There are now a few active nesting sites in the area that are reported. The John Bunker Sands Wetland Center has an active nesting site at the wetlands there. Take a look.

If you see a nesting site please report it to Texas Parks and Wildlife Department, also Audubon.

CHAPTER 5 - INFREQUENT AND UNUSUAL VISITORS

Black Swan *(Cygnus atratus)*

More than likely this visitor, from a few years back, was an escapee from a neighboring property. A pair of them frequented the lake for awhile. We imagine that the owners found out and came to take them home.

Black swans are native to Australia.

NATURE'S IMAGES *of* WHITE ROCK LAKE PARK

American White Pelican *(Pelecanus erythrorhynchos)*

Shout It Out

Interesting pose, don't you think? And just imagine what he is doing. Stretching? Swallowing? Or maybe both?

CHAPTER 5 - INFREQUENT AND UNUSUAL VISITORS

Ruby-crowned Kingley *(Regulus calendula)*

This Ruby-crowned Kinglet says we are done! So get out and have some fun! This is one bossy little bird. Noisy too! Guess we better listen!

Checklist

Start your own Journal of sightings here...

Be sure to include the date, time, weather conditions and the location in your notes. Write down what you observed the wildlife you are watching do - were they eating, sleeping, or taking a bath... well some of them do.

Make a note to yourself if you took a photograph or maybe drew a picture. Most of all have FUN! :)

Glossary

Aquatic – An organism that lives or grows in water

Camouflage – Ability to disguise or hide using foliage or patterns of coloration in animals and birds

Coloration – A genetically controlled pattern or markings that protects an individual organism

Crustaceans – An aquatic class of arthropods

Ecosystem – A system formed by the interaction of a community of organisms with their environment

Environment – The total of surrounding things, conditions or influences, including physical and biological factors

Fauna – A collective term for the animal life found in a habitat

Flora – A collective term for the plant life found in a habitat

Habitat – The immediate environment in which a plant or animal lives

Invasive – An intentionally or accidentally introduced non-native species that is brought into an ecosystem

Invertebrate – An animal which does not posses a backbone.

Marsupial – An animal that has a pouch for the receptacle of its young

Migration – The seasonal movement to pass from one region to another

Mimicry – The close resemblance of an animal to some different animal or to surrounding objects

Prairie – A tract of land mostly covered by specialized native grasses and forbs

Understory – The plants that grow in the areas under the canopy of trees

Urban – The area within a city

Wetland – Land or a low area of land that tends to be regularly or seasonally wet

Resources

TPWD Urban Biologists DFW Office

972-293-3841

911 Wildlife

214-368-5911

http://www.911wildlife.com

DFW Wildlife Coalition

972-234-9453

http://dfwwildlife.org/

National Bobcat Rescue & Research Foundation

972-567-3660

http://www.nbrr.org/

Rogers Wildlife Rehabilitation Center

972-225-4000

http://www.rogerswildlife.org/

Special Thanks

This is what we wrote early on…

The authors wish to thank our families and friends for their support and love.

Now it seems to be a tad bit on the short side of things, don't you think? For me personally there are a whole bunch of people that I would like to say thanks to, for their love, their time, their encouragement and for just being there.

Mom and Dad, now gone, but not forgotten. My son, what can I say, you have watched me go through a whole lot during your growing up years, teacher, naturalist, activist, the whole gambit. And you survived! Now grown and a graduate with your own degree, a good job and your own place to live. I am so proud of you and love you! What more could I ask for…. just call me every now and then ok, texting is getting old.

I would like to thank all those who inspired me to look in a different direction. Thanks to Mr. Hugh Freeman my high school AP Biology teacher whose stories of his summer expeditions opened my eyes to the world of butterflies and Dale Clark you are right there too. To David Hurt, business owner and birder extraordinaire whose indepth understanding of nature continues to amaze me. To Matt White and Jim Eidson for sharing their commitment to prairies, my special place. To the current and former TPWD Urban Biologists that I have known and respected for their continued interest in leading the way for others to understand this environment, Brett Johnson, Dr. Lou Verner and John Davis. A special thanks to a friend now gone but whom also loved his job, TPWD Game Warden Tom Carbone. Linda Sharp and Lennie Sutherland, I will remember our friendship and shared interests. And my White Rock friends, Ted and Hal Barker, Ben Sandifer, Robert Bunch, Kelly Cotten, Michael Jung, Susan Falvo, Kurt Kretsinger, Jeannie Terilli, Marci Gans Novak, and so many more who care about our lake. And a big thank you to a childhood friend, still friends after all these years, Mary Ann.

NATURE'S IMAGES *of* WHITE ROCK LAKE PARK

A special thanks to my brother Larry, who made me, umm encouraged me, to climb to the rim of Palo Duro Canyon way back when. We made it to the top and the view was spectacular. I can't thank you enough for all of your support and love brother.

This book would not have been possible without the friendship and shared love of White Rock with George Boyd and his wife Shirley. Words cannot express how lucky I was to meet them at the first Prairie Fest all those many years ago. Let's leave it at this; it was a true blessing when our paths crossed. Thank you.

Without the support and guidance of Mary Beth Smith this book would not have been possible. She led us, myself and Shirley, by the hand down the path of publishing and eased our anxiety. Yes, it was a process. We hope you will enjoy the results!

To all the friends who have taught and continue to teach me new things, given advice, listened and been there through the years, you know who you are and I am so grateful to each and every one of you. You are all amazing! Thank you!

I can't speak for George…but he liked to keep it simple. I am sure he would want to thank his "bride", Shirley. :)

ABOUT THE AUTHORS

George Boyd

George Boyd was a hunter and began his interest in birding by listening for the song of birds, then trying to identify them while he waited for game. As an avid runner he would pass by fields of grasses around the lake and hear different bird song and wonder which bird they belonged to. So began his quest, as he calls it, "my other hunting took place with a camera."

We all know that birds don't stay in one place too long so George began looking through a view-finder for them and learning how to use a camera. And the real hunt was on. George began taking photos not just of birds, but of any critter and flower he could, saying that his disease was growing. Becky called it just plain ol' curiosity. This also required a much bigger lens for George to take the best photos that he could. He is incredibly determined.

George added to the list of plants found at the lake by having their identification confirmed by the botanists with BRIT, especially Barney Lipscomb, and other experts. Those additions to the plant survey list occurred in the last 10 years of his dedication to the lake.

George defended our country in WWII while serving in the US Navy. After the war he attended Texas A&M on the GI Bill and graduated with his degree. After that he married his bride, Shirley, raised three sons and ran an international business located in Dallas.

Becky Rader

Becky Rader, wildlife biologist, naturalist and educator, has had a lifelong love for White Rock Lake, spending her childhood in the area. The sight of wildflowers being mowed while they were in bloom began the phone calls that would lead her to Larry Smith and Charlie Boseman, who were with DPARD at that time. That was the beginning of a positive involvement with DPARD for many years. This led to the TPWD Lone Star Land Steward Award in 2005.

The next step was educating the public about the existence of one of the rarest Blackland Prairies left, surviving in the middle of the city on thin soil over chalk rock. She planned a Prairie Fest each spring at the lake with several partnering organizations to spread the word. It took place for 6 years and that is where she met George, at the first Prairie Fest on a wildflower walk led by Jim Apken and Pat Hoyt, local Audubon members, who had been leading spring wildflower walks for the neighbors.

George learned he could now hunt wildflowers which led him to butterflies and dragonflies. A spring wildflower walk was the beginning of a wonderful friendship all because of a shared connection and love for the wonders of nature here in this special place, White Rock Lake Park, our oasis.

Becky taught for the Department of Defense Dependent Schools overseas and stateside, and taught in Dallas at private schools. She was a native plant and habitat consultant with a local organic landscape company and became the Chief Naturalist for the Dallas Museum of Natural History. She was appointed to the Environmental Health Commission by City Council representative, Sheffie Kadane and has served on several boards and has been involved in many

ABOUT THE AUTHORS

organizations, including North Texas Master Naturalist, Save Open Space, White Rock Lake Task Force and the Texas Association of Environmental Educators.

She has since become a consultant and was the lead consultant for the interpretive content for the John Bunker Sands Wetland Center in Seagoville. She has also consulted on other areas including prairie restoration, environmental education, and protection of wildlife habitat. This is her first book, but not her last.

Photo credit: Courtney Perry/The Dallas Morning News

Of Special Note

I had the extreme joy of working with my friend George and his wife Shirley on this book during what would be the last two months of George's life. It was a complete delight and led to many times when we were all laughing out loud at the stories he was telling us about one picture or the other. He had a lot of stories to tell, that was for sure. He was a generous man and had the kindest of hearts.

George was always eager to learn more, that is the fountain of youth you know, so he asked questions and sought out the people that could help him identify butterflies, like Dale Clark, or birds, like David Hurt, and so many others who stepped up and walked with him at the lake or just shared information with him. Many of those people became fast friends with George, who could resist that charm of his?

He assisted the St. John's Episcopal School students who asked if he would share some of his photos for their prairie studies. He did and talked to the students about the prairie, the birds, and butterflies and everything else that he saw. I don't know who enjoyed that more, George or the students.

I am so very thankful that this book was completed and had his approval before he left us all too soon.

He is missed by all who had the pleasure of knowing him.

Thank you George!

Becky

Made in the USA
Charleston, SC
18 February 2015